This book is dedicated to the whole wide world.Special
tribute to Queen Nataki for standing with a brutha.Salute
to my son Spuce Sinse' Shouts out to wedafamily,The
Panther Cubs,wefaus,usbeforeme,my entire family
and the whole hoodhopemovement tribe.

"The shame and the glory are misplaced"

PROPHET NOBLE DREW ALI

ISBN:9798459038422

Cover design by: HooodHope
Library of Congress Control Number: 2018675309
Printed in the United States of America

FOREWORD

I greet you in peace and it is my honor and pleasure to have my words before you.From being abused as a child and at one point forced to steal food so me, my mom and sister could eat.Then going in and out of juvenile detention centers,getting shot and going to adult facilities and finally serving 15 years wrongly convicted most of that time done in segregation(the hole)returning home to service the community working with various individuals to uplift ourselves from the block to the boardroom.Accepting full custody of my son,being homeless etc...
with all that said there is actually a lot more to this life I am living by grace,based on a true life story that begs to be told and tell it I will.That will be outlined in a book I will be publishing about my life called "True Tales of Trials and Tribulations"In the meantime and inbetween time here is a gem for the culture.Enjoy The Snitch nineFactor.

Thank you.

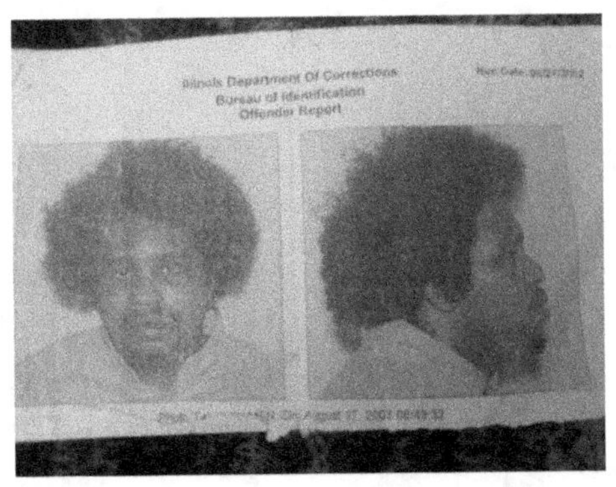
Illinois Department Of Corrections
Bureau of Identification
Offender Report
Run Date:

INTRODUCTION

Hello reader,my name is Brutha Hood the author of this book and the founder of Hoodhopemovement where our mission statement is to put a end to senseless violence and create economic opportunities in disenfranchised communities.We have been fulfilling our mission statement by partnering with Kwamae the owner of a tissue and papertowell manufacturing plant to provide everyday products to people.Also we are involved in street tribal truces and various levels of community service.Hoodhopemovement was founded while i was serving a 15 year sentence wrongly convicted.While inside the cages I penned several books and some have been published,among which include "The leadership factors"by B.Hood.Much of my awakening can be attributed to reading.I am convinced that it is of the utmost importance for those of us who have been gifted with insight regarding the ills that plague society to expose and express,remaining obligated to spread a message of healing.

Introducing Brutha Hood also known as B.Hood
to the ones not yet aware of this talented individual.Born and raised in Chicago in the trenches.

The leadership factors

By B. Hood

After serving 15 years wronly convicted,he returned to the communlty as a servant.Opened up youth centers and has been bootsontheground in Atlanta and phlladelphia to name a few.

Brutha Hood   founded Hoodhopemovement in 2010 while still serving time with the mission statement of ending senseless violence and creating economic oppoprtunity .
He has been consistent with the mission statement through community service music ,movies ,and books
Now you are invited to enjoy his latest ventures 'The snitch factor book and Nu song

for booking and interviews text 312-200-3555

The leadership factors
By B. Hood
amazon
Brutha Hood
ALSO KNOWN AS
B.Hood
Hoodhopemovement
MOVING MANUSCRIPTS, MOVIES &
MUSIC TO MOTIVATE
HOODHOPEMOVEMENT@GMAIL.COM
Popular releases
Nu Song
Latest Release • Single
Spotify
Singles and EPs
Nu Song
Who?
FROM XCON TO ICON
HOODHOPEMOVEMENT
BOOTSONTHEGROUND
TikTok
HOPE
MOVEMENT

PREFACE

This book is being published with the intentions of addressing the very serious issue of(to snitch or not to snitch) and what exactly snitching is,where did it originate from and what are the levels to it.

ALLOW THE RECORD
TO REFLECT

HOODHOPE

PROLOGUE

What is there to say that has not been said?
As society is evolving so are the issues.What I came to present here is a fresh perspective concerning snitching and the ramifications surrounding such.

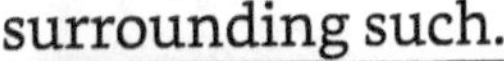

HOODHOPE IS THE MOVEMENT

K.W.D.E.
turn down 4 what
VIOLENCE
STOP THE
VIOLENCE

WE LOVE THE CHILDREN

THE SNITCH nine FACTOR

BY:MR.HOOD

Part:1

The Origin

For starters I would like to say that it was meant for me to draft this manuscript for the trials and tribulations that I was put through in this lifetime afforded me the experience sufficient to qualify me for such a powerful piece. The snitch Factory oops I mean the snitch Factor. Well, the snitch Factory would also be an appropriate term for the system has created a situation where snitches are required.

Information that I will be sharing within this book can be researched. I got the information from not simply books & videos but also being a jailhouse lawyer studying cases hearing countless tales of betrayal and moreover personal experience. Now I am sharing with hopes that these words will shed light on the culture.

My first experience with snitching came early. I did not grow up in the household where we were told to either confess your sins or turn on your family member. Just like any factor in life there are levels to snitching.

There are informants which is basically a spy, some work for the system and some work independently.

However, they both share the same agenda and that's personal gain. Self-preservation is considered the first law of nature.

When you consider another individual as yourself then betrayal is unlikely. (do unto others as you would have done unto you)

Let's go back in time for a better understanding or innerstanding.

This is not to debate the validity of the Holy Bible, but to highlight an instance of snitching in a very popular book.

In the book of genesis which is a Greek word meaning beginning.

In the beginning in the garden when Eve chose to listen to the whispers of a snake and entice Adam to also partake in the feast of apple delights. He willingly ate the Apple and when God appeared Adam immediately pointed the finger at Eve.

So, if you believe the Bible the first man was a snitch.

Previously I mentioned levels. There is the informant which is basically a spy and then the downright snitch which is considered betrayal. Eve apparently trusted Adam.

My first encounter with snitching began when I was about Ten running rampant in the streets of Chicago.

If mom was alive to read this book she would say "I knew it"

Me and few partners of mine had broken in a radio shack and grabbed some music equipment. Two of us got away one got caught.

Or at least I thought two of us got away.

I was staring out the window anxiously because we had split up.

I was waiting to see If he showed up at his house. It was late night and he had crept outside without permission later he would use the window to get back in. After sometime had passed and I had tapped on the window,

I went back to staring out the window. Low and behold the police pulled up. I was like aw damn the jig is up!

After they entered his building, they came back out,

came right across the street and grabbed me to the shock of my mother and Grandmother.

I had no record as a minor and was subsequently released from the police station.

After I took a shower,the stench of being betrayed still clouded my thoughts.

Back then I had never heard of snitching and could not define loyalty.

I instinctively felt a imbalance.I felt a injustice and at the same time not feeling a iota of remorse for depriving radio shack of their merchandise. Go figure.

Needless to say, that friendship was terminated. My next encounter with a snitchy situation would not come long after. Me and my cousin who was a year or two older than me got apprehended in a suburban part of Illinois for theft. I was not that worried but a part of me knew that the accumulation of petty offences would lead me to the Audy Home (juvenile detention Center).

At this point I had never been. Come to find out cuzo got a warrant. In the back of the squad car tells me he came up with an Alias, and "no matter what do not tell them my name.Stick with the alias and don't admit to nothing"

I was loyal and trustworthy and it never crossed my mind to rat cuz out. With regard to holding firm to innocence my young mind could calculate no way out when we were on camera and actually got caught with the merch.

Once we were taken to the police station we were separated and placed in separate bullpens

They came with all the tactics I would later become familiar with.Such as good cop bad cop, coupled with threats of more time or reward of less time. Although unfamiliar with the slick boy strategies I still held my ground. I gave my real name and it appeared I was headed to the Audy.

I recall the officer claiming that I would be raped once in there. In my mind I was thinking I would fight to the death if necessary. My homies who had been to juvie prior to me told very unpleasant stories.

None of rape.

Nevertheless, I held firm and kept telling them the name cuzo gave me. they returned to my cell several times saying"are you sure this is the name?

Are you positive?

Lying to a officer is a charge "and on and on but I kept with the name cuzo instructed. Later I discovered that the alias he conjured up was wanted for murder.

Unbeknownst to me at the time was that my cousin was being threatened and was under duress.

The officers expressed that not only did he fit the description of one wanted for murder,he had the same name.

while cuzo was insisting they had him mixed up, he broke down and gave up his government name.

Meanwhile when they came to question me concerning the name, I was consistent with the name he told me to tell them.

To this day me and him tell people that story and look back and laugh.

But it is not humorous at all when you are being confined for a substantial period of time based on word of mouth.

Part:2

The culture of the factor.

Culture is defined as:

the customs, arts, social institutions, and achievements of a particular nation, people, or other social group. That definition begs to ask the question

How did snitching or the no snitch policy become part of the culture. Such a factor was implemented as a result. Snitching is a verb; it is an effect.

Let's delve into the cause. With regard to history, some start with slavery while others go back farther before slavery, even as far back as the cosmos.

Slavery is often referred to as a reference point when dealing with the ills of modern-day society due to the brainwashing of names and language replaced with something foreign and religious ideas forced upon a people.Just to list a few of the atrocities that transpired.And tragic as it is,some forms of the truama are ongoing.

Such a dramatic experience has Caused a ripple effect and some remaining drowning in a pool of misdirection based on lack of identity.

Snitching is the act of turning someone in to authority figures basically the police. But it gets deeper

There is dry snitching and just outright snitching.

Make mental note that I just mentioned the police in connection with the snitch factor being a part of the culture. For the two are closely related and share a vested interest.

Some individuals imagine a utopia,which is a perfect society where crime does not exist.

However, such individuals that are born with negative energy exist. For example, look at the rap industry as murderous behavior and who can do the most harm to another human being is glorified. Even before hip hop such a savage lifestyle is indicated in wars and slavery.

Art imitates life and at times life imitates art.

Before we proceed further let's elaborate

On what exactly is snitching? And what is dry snitching? The origin of snitching began with the formation of a police.

The police originated on the slave plantation. They were slave catchers. One of the tactics they would apply is to punish other slaves when another slave escaped.

They would even torture children in order to convince the slaves to rat out a fellow slave.

Even when I was incarcerated if one inmate did something,Even if they apprehended the individual or individuals who committed the infraction the officer\overseer would punish us all.

This tactic would cause division and instigate a situation where inmates would challenge each other based on institutional rules.

Because inmates had their own set of rules as well.

Dry snitching is indirect snitching. For example, let's say its two people in the car and the police pull you over.

There is a gun under the seat it is not yours. The police discover said weapon and ask who this belongs to?

You belt out "it's not mine" that is considered dry snitching. On the flip side of that is the fact of this person not taking their own weight is also a form of dry snitching.

The end result are the actions or inactions of someone else leads to another or others being captured,or issued some degree of discipline/punishment. The snitch factor has evolved over time and taken a certain place in the culture.

Part:3

The Naked Truth

The origin of snitching allows understanding into the current factors.

At some point any slave or (field slave) in particular that communicated with the oppressors were considered traitors.

Unless they were spies for the field slaves that worked their way into the slave masters house, to be labeled as house slaves.

I recall when I was behind bars if internal affairs called you to their office you had to refuse to go and accept a disciplinary ticket for "disobeying a direct order"

Or another inmate witness must be allowed To accompany you. If you chose to go to internal affairs office unaccompanied then you came back to the cell house at your own risk.

The part about the field slave and the house slave

Is key to unlocking the understanding of snitching itself and why the factor even exists.

At one point if any of the field slaves communicated with the slave masters, they were considered traitors unless

They were a spy on behalf of the field slaves. Basically, if there were no slave catchers then there would be nothing to snitch on.

Ok fast forward to the current snitch factor. The slogan "snitches get stiches" grew very popular, surely you have heard the saying.

The difference in the shift of the factor from the slave plantation and the invention of the police

In comparison to current times is simply the invention of crime. Yes, crime was invented. Documented proof exists of the government delivering narcotics and weapons into the ghetto.

The real Rick Ross not the rapper was reported as making one million dollars a week bringing crack cocaine into the hood. Who was he working for? The C.I.A

The central intelligence agency. This is all public information. Also, public information is the fact they started the counterintelligence program or cointelpro

To spy on organizations and leaders that were involved in efforts to uplift the community. Prime example The honorable Chairman Fred Hampton Sr. The leader of the Black Panther Party in Chicago during the 60s, was assassinated by Chicago police December 4th 1969 based on information provided to the government from the counterintelligence program utilizing a spy they hired by the name of William O'Neil. He is just one of the ones we are aware of.

So, there you have it with the invention of crime grows a need for police. Because beside raving maniacs which are rare the police basically protect the people who have from the ones that have not. Most crime besides crimes of passion and crimes of revenge, are committed for material gain.

Recently The rapper styles P from the group The Lox made a viral video explaining the snitch culture.

He was explaining the

Differences between what is described as a civilian (a person not involved in crime) and a street person. He mentioned that a civilian is not governed by the same rules or G code that the streets abide by. In other words, if a civilian is violated, they basically have no other recourse than to involve law enforcement.

While I was incarcerated, I made an observance.

The actual act of snitching is the violation of trust. Because it constitutes betrayal and disloyalty at a high height.

Criminals share an unwritten bond to be sworn enemies of law enforcement period.

When that bond is broken to betray another criminal, it is a selfish act.

People who are not involved in crime or the street life have no obligations to the G Code, or sworn secrecy, they are not declared to be enemies of law enforcement.

Also, while doing time inmates were not allowed to prey on the weak or run to the officers. (Some of our rules) And I realize that portion of the factor is missing in the hood today.

The no snitch rule existed for two important reasons.

Number 1: we could not trust the police in the community.

 Number 2: We policed our ourselves.

As indicated, the first reason still exists, however the second rule, not so much.

And that is one problem.

The other problem is the fact that not only does crime exist, but crime worth reporting is being committed continuously.

That says a lot about society. Hence a utopian society does not exist to my knowledge. I have read that in Israel there is a community, built by Ben Amin from Chicago, of Hebrews where there exist no crime and no diseases, and where they honor a vegan diet.

However, they still have laws. Law and order go together one does not exist without the other.

Law and order are required in a civilized

Society. Some people of today have made proud claims to being a savage and/or being on demon time. A direct indication that order is mandatory.

The law in the community attempting to restore order are out of order themselves. For instance, there are officers with several complaints that have been promoted in rank and given raises. What other job besides the police department can you get a raise and promotion after compiling numerous complaints?

This is all at the tax payers' expense and that is what is meant by defunding the police. It is a clear and present danger in the sense of disorder,subsequently law is necessary.

These officers with such horrendous records not only cost tax payers by way of their nearly hundred thousand dollar a year salary but also lawsuits filed for police brutality or police murder.

PART 4:

The solution

I personally feel that in the community many times the issues or problems that plague the community are dwelled on or expounded upon but not enough energy is given to the solution.

The solution is obviously stop doing crime if you don't like dropping dimes,because informants, spies and snitches are an intricate portion of the street game. Accurately described in some hoods as "the trap"

Another solution is for the community to police themselves. This tactic of the community policing themselves has proven to be effective.

 Before I end this most needed discussion outlined in this book regarding the snitch factor, I would like to share a story with you.

 I recall one time while I was incarcerated, I was watching a show called mob wives.

It was kind of gangster,but the main attraction for me was the women. Being separated from the opposite sex greatly exaggerates one's desire.

Anyhow in this particular episode the wife of Sammy the bull (a famous mafia snitch) was present at the table.

Sammy the bull most likely played a role in Their husbands incarceration or subsequent demise based on information he provided to the federal law enforcement.

The conversation they were having was quite interesting. Important to note that Sammy the Bull snitched on the leader of the mafia John Gotti.

This was after hearing a recording of a wiretap the feds played for the bull with Gotti saying some nasty things about him etc.

 Same scenario played out in snitch nine case because they played a recording of Jim jones and another affiliate discussing his fate and this caused him to fold and work with authorities. Now back to the episode of mobwives.

The discussion the wives and girlfriends were having intensified as the women were degrading Sammy for his acts of treachery and betrayal,with regard to his testimony incriminating mob members.

I was nodding silently in agreement with such criticism. For I myself was incarcerated at the time as a result of street dudes coming to court on me. (Looking back, I can see that it was done for me not to me) More on that subject in my next book "true tales of trials and tribulations"

Now as I am mentally absorbing this dialogue from the television show

Something caught my ear.

The wife of Sammy the Bull spoke up and replied saying that they, the other wives, were proud of husbands who were murderers whom took family members away from people family.

 But her hubby Sammy the bull (also a murderer for he admitted to five murders that he said john Gotti instructed him to do)he was snitching on other murderers to get back to his family. Which one is worse? Murder or snitching?

I suppose it depends on who you ask. Prophet Noble Drew Ali said

The glory and the shame are misplaced.

Hope you enjoyed this book. There is more to come. You can google hoodhopemovement

A Bootsontheground organization I founded after serving 15 years incarcerated. Antwan Alexander on Facebook unless they purge that page too for me being a truth teller. Instagram hoodhope and

Hoodhopemovement check for hoodhopemagazine on facebook & HoodHope on facebook

And youtube.

. As a Courtesy to the readers, I have taken the liberty of including excerpts from one of my upcoming children

books.

Bonus coverage for the people who purchased the hard back.I am including a piece I penned while incarcerated entitled The Gangstah factor.

CHAPTER 1

learning to cope without Mr. Owl was a wise bird about the world, he was a friend to every little boy

and girl.

The children would listen whenever he would talk,

 but they wonder why he would always walk.

Here and there he would stroll while his friends would fly,so one day a child named Prince asked him

"why?"

Mr.Owl stared and scratched his head,

 which caused Prince to repeat what he just said. "Mr.Owl

can you tell us why you don't fly?"

 "oh how I yearn to soar the sky" he said"far above the mountains high

with the wind in my ears and the clouds in my eyes. The great question that has been asked a thousand

times instead of sitting on top of Georgia Pines I am perched on the bush so low to the ground"

"woo woo"

came the familiar sound it was two other Owls whizzing by, they appear to be sailing across the sky.

Mr. Owl just walked and never missing a step, he said "Prince it has been two days since I slept."

" Why Mister

have you not rested your eyes ?is that the reason why you cannot fly?"

"No Prince it is no such thing, I have

lost my wings." So, Prince began to look here,

 he looked there, he looked up he looked down he looked

everywhere.Then he asked the rabbit he asked the worm in the ground, he asked the turtle the butterfly" have

you see Wings Around?"

"oh no they said we have seen them not, but if we find them I will tell you "replied the fox.

Mr.Owl looked sad and that's when Prince turn to say, "I don't have wings and I still play! We Run

skip trip hop tuck flip kick and fall, Mr. Owl we even talk while we walk, we can do it all." moral to the story if

you can't find the means to get by and walk across the sky then allow your mind to fly.

CHAPTER 2

No gangs

Today Mr. Owl traveled alone in the park.

The sun was going down it was just getting dark.

Mr. Owl was with another owl friend having a discussion, when all of a sudden,several vultures came

rushing.

Mr.Owl and his friend were very brave, and the vultures could see they were not afraid.

Mr. Owl

was a enemy to none, man or bird,

but he and the vultures had once exchanged unpleasant words.

They often ganged up on his other friends of the sky,

 so one day he asked the vultures why?

They replied.

"Because we can and you are a outsider if you not with us,

Plus we must prove we are tough."

Mr.Owl was friendly and never like to fuss

He bid the vultures farewell and left in a rush.

The next day they met again and the vultures once again were not friendly at all,

In fact, it appeared to Mr. Owl that they wanted to brawl. "Listen here you vultures" said Mr. Owl

"Fighting is not my style"

Mr. Owl went on to say

"It has become clear to me that this group,

Chooses to bully and behave as brutes."

One of the vultures leaned over and whispering in Mr. Owls Ear the vulture said

 "join us and you will have nothing to fear."

Another vulture said "if everything we

heard so far is true,

Then we could use a bird like you"

Mr.Owl replied "what have you heard? "

One of the vultures said." we heard that you are wise"

Then Mr. Owl told them "Then you should know I am smart enough not to join with you

guys"

"I think it is dumb to pick on people for fun"

A vulture shoved Mr. Owl and told him they were like family, sisters and brothers, there to assist and

defend each other.

"I am not a bird of that feather "said Mr. Owl

"As I stated before fighting is not my style"

As the vultures moved in closer. Mr. Owl began speaking. He said "it makes no sense attacking me you

have no reasoning.

In some way we are all connected, and all species should be respected. To cause harm to

me would cause harm to you,"

The vultures paused confused about what to do,

because what Mr. Owl said was true.

After forming a group huddle the vultures told Mr. Owl, he was right,

 and vowed from that day not to

bully or start fights.

The end.

Another learning tool streaming on all platforms is a song called "Who" by:Brutha Hood

S KEELER AV

Antwan Alexander
Say less

JMD REAL DEEP BLAQ ICE
HOOD HOPE
MAGAZINE
PUT THEM
GUNS
DOWN!!!
BOOTSONTHE
GROUND
#HooHope

BRUTHA HOOD

Mr.HoodHope himself,
Mondrea Vining born in the 70s in Chicago Illinois. He was raised without his father and at a early age got involved with the street life and became swallowed up in tribal warfare and criminal culture. His transformation was similar to the Malcolm Little to Malcolm X conversion.
He founded HoodHopeMovement in 2010 with the mission of ending senseless violence and creating economic opportunities in disenfranchised communities.
This journey has allowed him to function as head administrator of several locations geared toward rescuing at risk youth.
HoodHopeMovement has partnered with several organizations,churches,centers,mosques,and various politicians in efforts to seek solutions to the violence that plagues the inner city.
Many know him as "Real Deep" the associate editor and publisher of the Chicago street journal formerly known as south street journal.
He is a board member of golden points and The Catherine Smith foundation.
Highly regarded in grassroots circles based on close ties with many veteran and up and coming community activists.This man is connected in the streets and boardrooms of Chicago.If you know him then you know that his authenticity is never in question and that his drive is focused entirely on the goodwill of us. If you do not know him and you are interested in saving lives contact him 312-785-4182.

JUSTICIA MIGRANTE
Ben & Jerry's
Human Rights
Cannot Wait!
MIGRANT
JUSTICE
Sign The
Milk with Dignity
Program Now!
HOODHOPE

HONK YOUR
HORN TO SHUT
THIS STORE
DOWN
SHOP WHERE YOUR
LIFE AND DOLLARS
MATTER!
You're
choking
me!

32

H O P E
MOVEMENT
HELPING SELF SUFFICIENCY UNITED
Easy Fella

4 YEARS AGO

H★★D
H♥P E
MOVEMENT
REACHING SELF SUFFICIENCY UNITED
It Takes
The Hood
To Save
The Hood
TOTAL

UNCLENEPH
HOODHOPEMOVEMENTS

HOODHOPEMOVEMENT
ONTHEGROUND

The Final Call
NETFLIX
Farrakhan
& Controversy

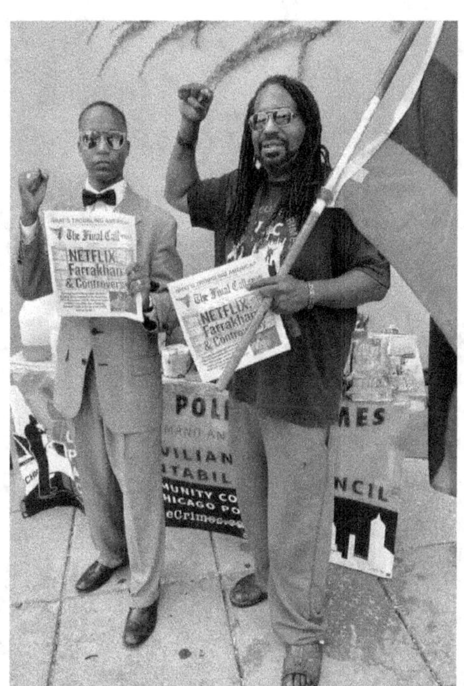

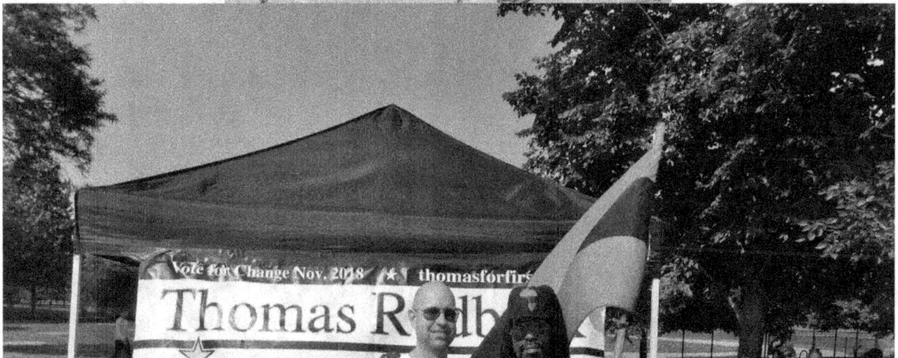
Vote for Change Nov. 2018
Thomas
Rudbeck
★ Creating Jobs ★ Stopping Viole

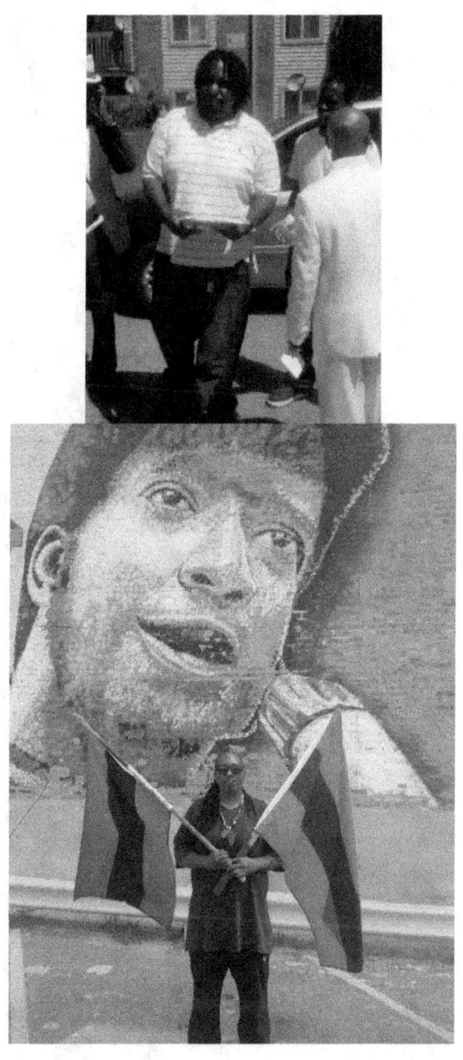

TISSUE IS THE ISSUE

Support
High Quality Tissue
From the
Community Based
Business Alliance
(C.B.B.A)

HOODHOPEMOVEMENT
312-200-3555

RESTAURANT
OPPORTUNITIES
CENTER OF CHICAGO

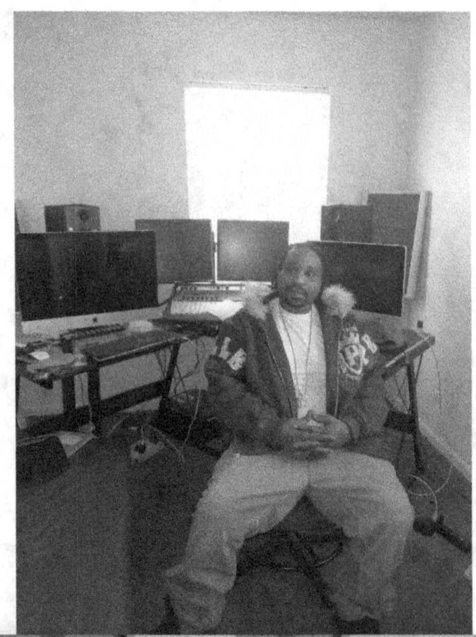

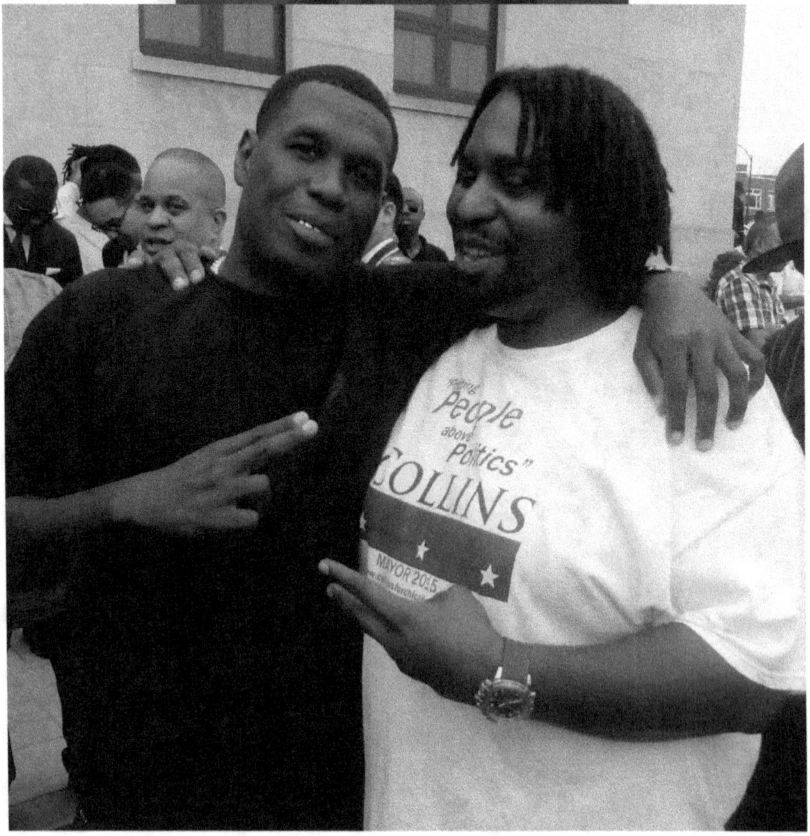
People
above
Politics"
COLLINS
MAYOR 2015

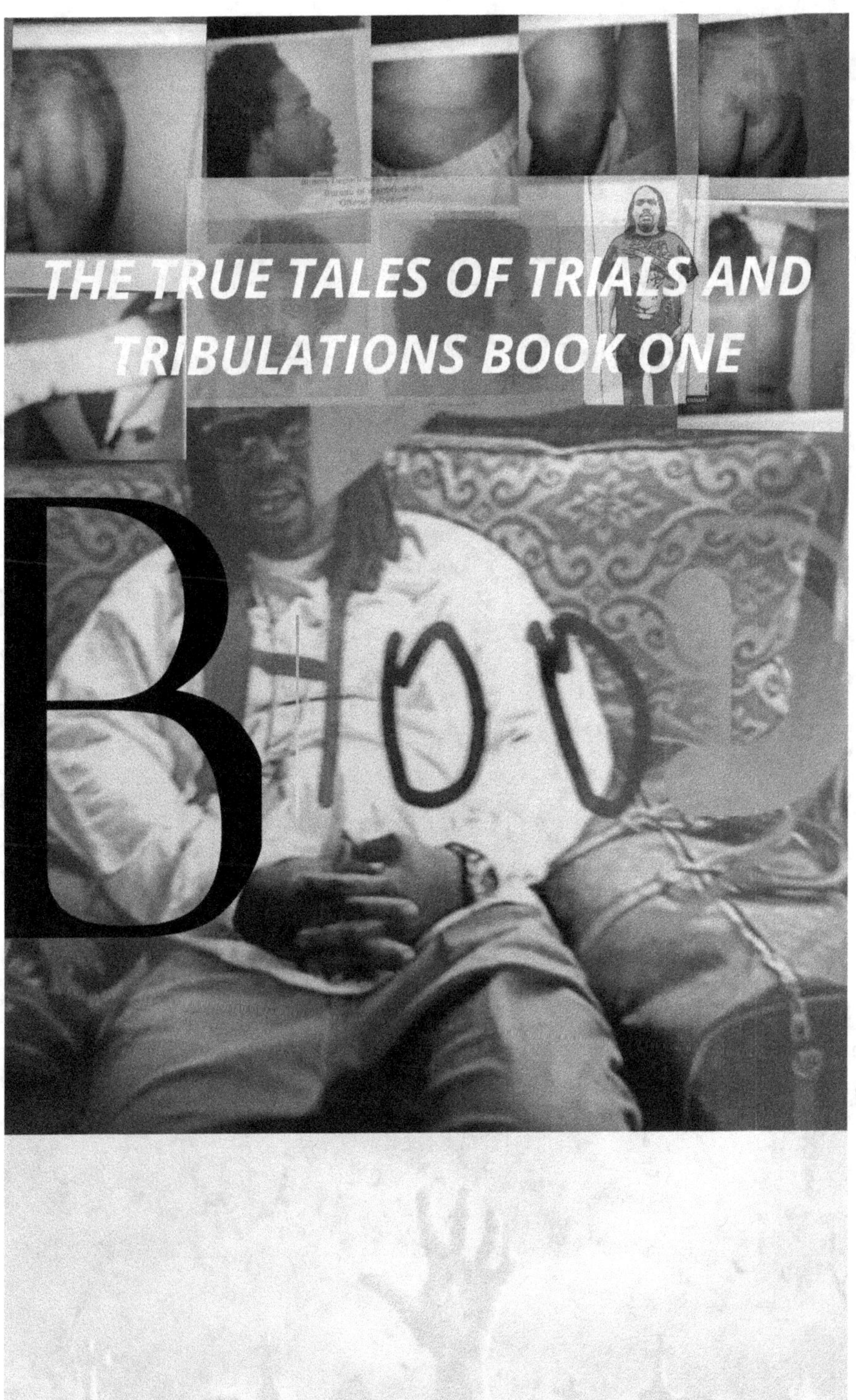
THE TRUE TALES OF TRIALS AND TRIBULATIONS BOOK ONE
B OO

I AM
THE C.H.A. WAITLIST
I AM
SCHOOLS

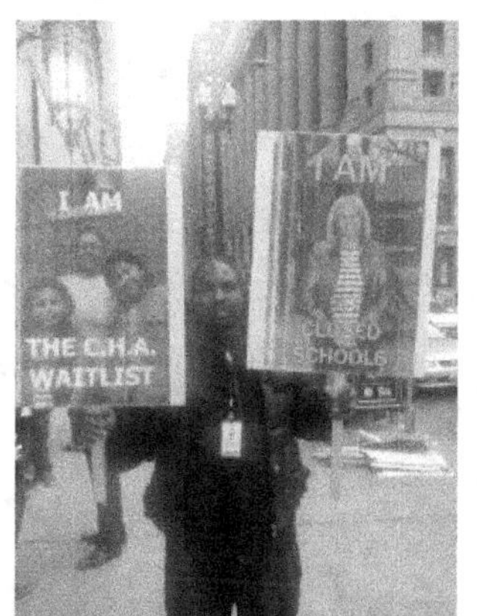

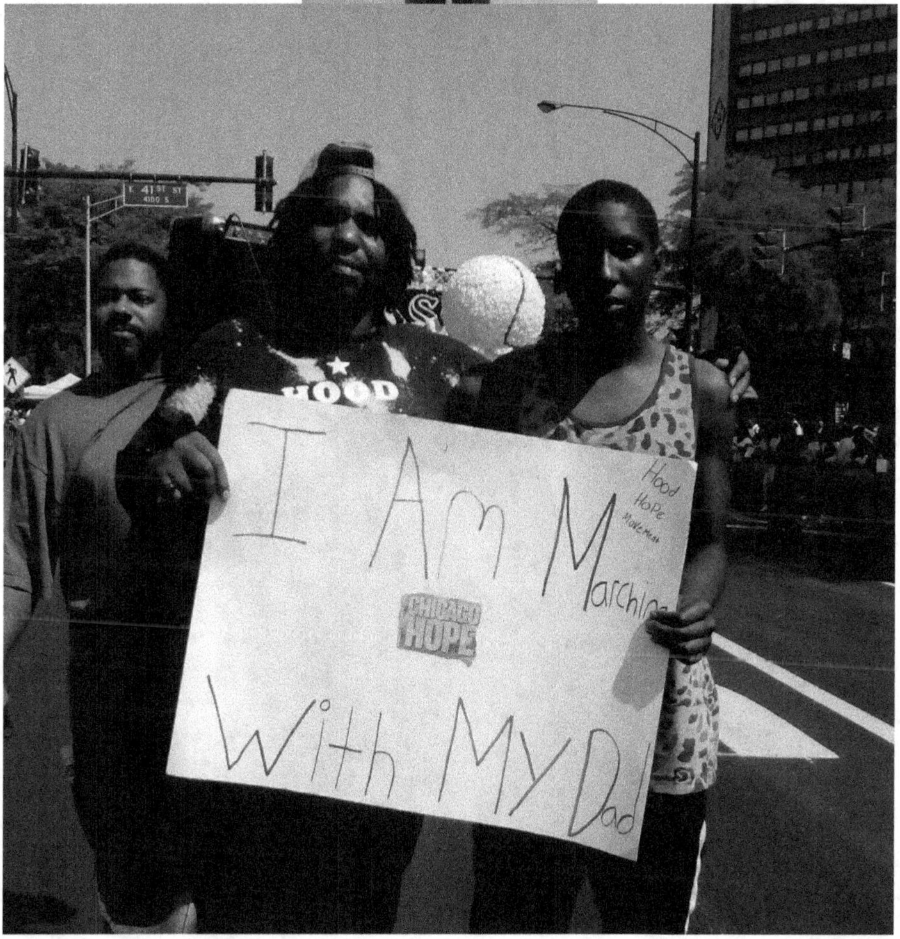
E 41ST ST
4100 S
HOOD
I Am Marching With My Dad!
Hood Hope Movement
CHICAGO HOPE